# *The Prestige S....*
# **Ribble**

### John Banks
### Photography by G H F Atkins

*Cover:* Number **1863** (**ARN863C**) was a 1965 Albion Lowlander with Alexander 72-seat bodywork. It was photographed at Bolton in September 1969.

*Rear cover:* A colourful Ribble timetable from 1932. *(Keith Healey Collection)*

*Title page:* Fully fronted, front-engined double-deckers were fairly numerous, but two fleets - Southdown and Ribble - made of them an art-form. Southdown's PD3s are among the most famous of postwar traditional buses; if Ribble's suffered in the comparison at all, it was only through having a somewhat duller livery: mostly dark-red with very little cream relief. Perhaps the somewhat austere lines of the MCCW or Burlingham bodywork told against them, too. This view is of a Burlingham example, No. **1596** (**LCK759**) of 1958. *(Senior Transport Archive)*

*Opposite page:* The Ribble "White Lady" was something quite new in the late 1940s. Double-deck coaches were not unknown, but there had been few, and fewer successful ones, up to that time. Number **1203** (**BRN263**), a Leyland PD1/3 Titan with Burlingham lowbridge 49-seat coachwork, had entered service as fleet number 2520 in 1948. In this March 1951 view it was at Lower Mosley Street coach station, Manchester, about to leave for Blackburn on the X66 Manchester to Blackburn service purchased from L Cronshaw in 1937 jointly with Lancashire United Transport and Bolton Corporation. Conditions were very dull, and the photographer has recorded that an exposure of a half-second was necessary, with the camera supported on a convenient wall.

*Below:* Front-line coaches from the former British Electric Traction and Transport Holding Company fleets were painted white in National Bus Company ownership. It was just about possible to make out an operational case for having a nationwide corporate livery for express vehicles, despite the vast amounts of goodwill the old company names and colours could, and did, command. So it was that the Leylands, AECs, Bristols and the rest, in their characteristic liveries, went into the melting pot and emerged in the NBC's less than imaginative colour scheme. The damage done by this exercise was tacitly admitted when the old company fleetnames were allowed, in small letters, as secondary identities for a while. This group of Ribble coaches thus turned out was at Bowness-on-Windermere in May 1974. Numbers **955** (**HRN955G**), **956** (**HRN956G**), **875** (**ECK875E**), **791** (**ARN791C**), and **733** (**TRN733**) are visible. They were all Plaxton-bodied Leyland Leopards dating from the 1960s.

X66
BLACKBURN

RIBBLE

1203

BRN 263

**RIBBLE**

# Introducing

# R I B B L E

OPERATORS OF FIRST-CLASS
INCLUSIVE COACH TOURS
THROUGHOUT BRITAIN

Ribble was one of the great ones, a giant in the British Electric Traction camp: it still exists, under the aegis of the Stagecoach and Blazefield organisations, but this book sets out unashamedly to celebrate the Ribble of the classic period when, in the Company's prime, its dark-red and cream buses and coaches could be seen in most parts of the country from Glasgow to Plymouth and from the seaside in the west to the shores of the East Coast.

The majority of the photographs used are from the legendary G H F Atkins collection. Geoffrey Atkins started recording the Ribble fleet in the early 1930s and his work from then until the advent of the National Bus Company in 1969 has provided a mouth-watering coverage from which our selection is made. Where Geoffrey missed recording a particular feature of the fleet, judicious additions from the equally renowned Senior Transport Archive fill the gaps.

Readers of earlier volumes in this series will know that Geoffrey Atkins has a quite specific aim when taking his photographs, and that is to provide himself with a visual record of the art of the coachbuilder. Coachwork is his prime interest and often a single exposure has sufficed to give him a satisfactory record. In the prewar period, his skill at producing such photographs was - as he will cheerfully admit - honed by the need to make every exposure count at a time when money for hobbies was at a premium. To some extent the same exigencies are responsible for the preponderance of nearside-front views in Geoffrey's work. Part of his requirement is to show the platform and entrance arrangements as well as the position of the staircase. On British, right-hand-drive vehicles, the nearside-front angle gives all these, as well as the radiator and

bonnet-line on traditional vehicles, the whole adding up to the best method of recording the coachbuilder's work.

The writer is privileged to have been regarded as a friend of Geoffrey's for more than three decades, and the opportunity to get to know his matchless collection (apart from the intrinsic pleasure it has given) has shown that, in cases of favourite types, two or more views were taken and - further - that a fair number of traffic and general scenes featuring public service vehicles have been taken, as has a superb, unparalleled series of after-dark shots. In the postwar period, including a change to the more economical 35 millimetre format, this process has continued and has produced, overall, a collection that, in the writer's opinion, has no equal. One area in which it certainly is without equal is the timespan: the first picture was taken in 1927, the latest earlier this year (2001 - though not in this volume). To have thus taken transport photographs in each of nine consecutive decades must surely be a record.

There is often, too, a slight but most attractive "off-beat" element to Geoffrey's photography, in that an operator's fleet will be depicted in less obvious locations. Major operators' coaches, for example, might be featured away from their main operating areas, in such locations as Ilfracombe or Llandudno, Skegness or Scarborough: these and others were all holiday destinations for the Atkins family. And therein lies one of the secrets of success of the GHFA Collection: the pictures were taken in odd moments during life's normal activities. Geoffrey has never been one to rush round bus stations or garages snapping everything in sight regardless of position or lighting conditions. Many shots were unplanned, true, and have a consequent delightful spontaneity; but those that were are frequently cases of Art concealing Art, for the planning and composition are so meticulous and skilful that the results scarcely ever seem contrived.

To have such a photographer turn his attention to a fleet such as that of Ribble, therefore, is a matter for celebration, and once again the writer and publisher offer their thanks to Geoffrey for so readily making his best work available for another *Prestige Series* album.

What was it about Ribble? What caused its immense, loyal following among several

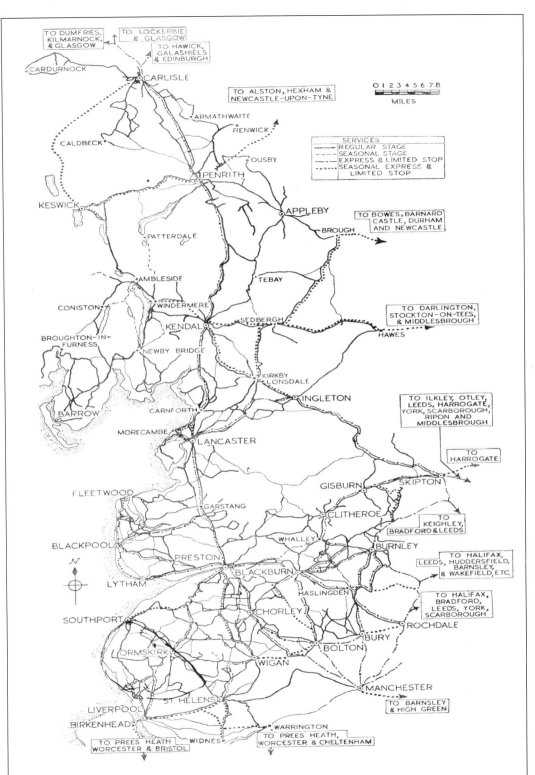

*Under the heading "Bus Advertising Pays", this map was presented to potential advertisers in 1957 by the British Electric Traction Federation Ltd. It revealed a substantial operating area which saw Ribble vehicles on the roads between Glasgow and Cheltenham; Barrow and Middlesbrough. (Keith Healey Collection)*

*In the pre-Lion era, that is in the first half of the 1920s, the Leyland bus was a rather ungainly creature compared with the elegant designs which the late twenties and the thirties would bring. It was a sound, practical vehicle, nonetheless, which found favour in many fleets; at that time, indeed, the seeds of some very long-lived operator/maufacturer relationships were sown. Ribble, for example, bought its first Leyland - an SG7 very much like No. **67 (CK3532)** of 1923 pictured above - in 1922 and was still buying them more than six decades later. (Senior Transport Archive)*

generations of enthusiast? It was one of the earliest fleets to have a cohesive identity, for it was incorporated in 1919 in the immediate aftermath of the Great War. Its roots can be traced even further back, however, to the business begun in 1910 by Mr J Hodson, of Gregson Lane, Preston. For almost a decade matters proceeded in a small way and by the end of the War Mr Hodson was running a mere five vehicles. In that first full year of peace, Mr Hodson made a business arrangement with Major H E Hickmott, as a consequence of which his business was reconstituted as Ribble Motor Services Limited. Major Hickmott was appointed Managing Director, a post he was to hold for a quarter-century until his retirement in 1944. Mr Hodson was a director of the new company.

As might have been expected, the proximity of the Company's headquarters to those of Leyland Motors Limited quickly produced a close working relationship. New vehicles in the period 1919 - 1923 came from AEC, Daimler and Vulcan and it took the salesmen from Leyland a couple of years or so to land their first order - for a single-deck SG7 type in 1922. For the next two decades the Company bought very few new chassis of any other make: a handful of small Dennises and some AEC Regals for the associated Standerwick fleet. In the war years, as with many another operator not used to such

things, austerity Daimlers and Guy Arabs entered the fleet by dint of Ministerial Decree. From 1946, however, and for more than two decades, orders were once again directed towards Leyland Motors and a vast and steady restocking took place, interspersed with penny numbers of Sentinels, Albion Lowlanders and Bedfords, until, in 1968/9, orders were placed for Bristols, both single- and double-deck. As the National Bus Company began to make its mark, following its inauguration on 1st January 1969, Bristols held their own with Leylands in the Ribble fleet for a decade until suppressed by their new owner - none other than Leyland. Thereafter Leyland Nationals and Olympians continued the tradition into a later era beyond the remit of this book.

Inevitably, the acquired fleet told a different story. At the very outset, Mr Hodson contributed four Karriers and a Leyland and during the remainder of the prewar years *marques* coming into the care of Ribble's engineering staff included ADC, Albion, Bean, Bristol, Burford, Chevrolet, Crossley, Dennis, Dodge, Fiat, Gilford, GMC, Guy, Halley, Laffley, Maudslay, Minerva, Morris, Overland, Pagefield, Reo, Republic, Saurer, Thornycroft and TSM: a situation that doubtless gave the engineers many a headache.

This veritable gallimaufry of more or less exotic non-Leyland *marques* was perhaps to be

*Company "ephemera" has, in a gratifyingly large number of cases, proved anything but ephemeral. Many examples have survived, cheaply printed on flimsy paper as they may be, to tell us what the bus and coach operators were doing, almost on a day-to-day basis, in their heyday. These two leaflets from the mid 1930s advertised tours and "land cruises" and, as might be expected, the vehicles doing the work were Leylands. (Keith Healey Collection)*

expected. In the 1920s, independent operators abounded and were usually highly distinctive, not to say peculiar, in their vehicle preferences. In the few years from Ribble's first acquisition of a competing operator, in 1923, up to the end of 1931, over 50 were acquired either wholly or jointly with, for example, United Automobile Services Limited. In true "big company" fashion, however, the majority of the non-standard vehicles were quickly sold off, sometimes without being repainted or even operated.

There were also, of course, bearing in mind the geographical spread of the acquired competitors' operating areas, many Leylands among the second-hand acquisitions and, in general, these fitted in with the existing fleet and worked for a number of years before being withdrawn. So Leyland and Ribble became synonymous and for several decades it would have been quite unthinkable for the Company to place orders elsewhere.

And this is how many a busman, and many an enthusiast (some people were both, of

course), including the writer, saw the Company. In his case it was discovered during trips from the family home in East Yorkshire to the Lake District and across to Blackpool. A reversion to the immodesty of the first person is needed, however, to describe how the Ribble fleet became for the writer a legend in its own lifetime.

I left school in 1958 and took a clerical job in a local factory's administration offices. In 1959 I went on the first holiday I had ever spent free of parental control - a summer week in a Blackpool boarding house. There was a lot to fit in during that week. There was the search for out-of-the-way shops for unusual, second-hand gramophone records, which even in my teenage years was a bit of an obsession; there were the pubs and dance halls into which my office friend and I slunk, despite being slightly under-age (at least for the former); there were the inevitable visits to Blackpool Tower and the various funfairs on the Golden Mile (the craze to "collect" rides on ever bigger Ferris Wheels and better Big Dippers was then just starting);

there was the chance (really!) meeting with a young lady, holidaying with her parents in the next door boarding house, from my home town - the parents were pleased that I seemed willing (I was!) to take their daughter off their hands for several evenings and afternoon excursions; there were ...

But what about the transport? What about Ribble? I can hear impatient readers muttering. Well, there were the trams; there was the Coliseum coach terminal. And there was Ribble. In 1959 the passenger-carrying industry was not yet fully into the doldrums caused by those twin advances (or regressions, it might be argued) of civilisation: television and mass car ownership. Thus municipal and company operators still commanded satisfactory loadings in their urban operating areas at most times of the day, and private hire and excursion traffic was - at least in Blackpool - a sight to behold.

I recall writing down many hundreds of fleet and associated registration numbers during that week, a significant quantity of them belonging to Ribble Leylands and a miscellany of operators working on hire to Ribble. Today, I often curse the fact that I took no photographs in the fifties: never more so than when recalling that week in Blackpool.

I did not own a camera. The family did. It was an ancient Kodak Vest Pocket, which was known to let light in through the bellows. I had used it the previous summer during a three-week school-exchange visit to France. Photographs taken included some at the Brussels World Fair and some in Paris. The result was a set of tiny, dismal, wretched disappointments, parentally financed to the accompaniment of much grumbling, which have not survived. I could not fund the purchase of a new apparatus. Well, the boarding house alone was £5.19.6d for the week, then there were the coach fare, a reasonable amount for meals and evening conviviality, entrance fees ... And my weekly wage then was £3.5s.0d.

Accordingly, the memory has to serve as the photograph album for that particular week. Long lines of cream and dark-red (we always called it maroon, though I believe that to be inaccurate) coaches, as well as reversed-liveried service buses standing in during the summer seasonal rush, are vivid in the mind's eye. As are dozens of independents' coaches and not a few less-than-pristine service buses with "On Hire to Ribble" stickers in the front windows. The only comparable experience I can bring to mind is standing on an overbridge across the A1 as it ran (then) into London on Cup Final Day in 1961, watching an unending stream of coaches heading for Wembley Stadium.

All too soon this kind of seaside spectacular, which had waxed gloriously and begun already to wane in the decade following the end of the Second World War, was to fade even further and eventually be eclipsed by queues of motor cars which served, and still serve, little purpose, it seems, other than to frustrate their occupants who cannot get to where they wish to be, as well as preventing the passage of those public service vehicles that remain in business.

Albeit not in Blackpool, that era and its more distant counterpart of the thirties are splendidly evoked in this series of images from the camera of Geoffrey Atkins, ably aided and abetted as acknowledged.

The usual disclaimer - that this book is neither a history nor a fleet list - is more apposite, perhaps, than usual, when dealing with an enormous fleet and operation such as Ribble's was in the classic period.

The regularity of the writer's thanks to fellow enthusiasts Ron Maybray and Philip Battersby should not be taken as a mechanical response. As has been stated before, it is unlikely that these books would be publishable without their having kept this scribbler on the straight and narrow. Readers will also be well used to the writer's grateful recognition directed towards the PSV Circle and The Omnibus Society, whose publications are of such immense help to anyone setting out to produce a volume such as this. Other essential publications have been the two volumes written by T B Maund and Alan Townsin published by Venture Publications in 1993 and 1994. Grateful thanks also to the British Commercial Vehicle Museum for courteously allowing reproduction of Leyland material held in the Senior Transport Archive.

On this occasion, too, as with the recent volume on North Western, both John Senior and Keith Healey have contributed notably to the accuracy of the text. Roy Marshall has kindly read the final draft and made a number of useful amendments. David and Mary Shaw have yet again given of their time to proofread the completed work and have saved the writer from the embarrassment of seeing a number of typing errors in print.

*John Banks,*
*Romiley, Cheshire.*
*April 2001*

Ribble was a most avid collector of competing businesses in the second half of the 1920s. Pilgrim Motors (T E Smith), of Elswick, fell in July 1927, contributing a mixed fleet of nine vehicles. Two of the nine were Leylands, which fitted in well with Ribble's Leyland philosophy. Whereas the ex-Pilgrim Vulcans and a Dodge were withdrawn quite quickly, the Leylands lasted into the 1930s: a PLSC1 Lion until 1938 and this C7, No. **351 (TD3854)**, until 1932. It was photographed in Preston on 25th August 1931 after an overhaul and repaint. (*Senior Transport Archive*)

The Leyland Leveret, generally with 20 seats, was Leyland's "small" bus until the advent of the Kingston-built Cub. Ribble's No. **940** (**TD6477**) came from the Furness Omnibus Company Limited, of Dalton-in-Furness, in May 1930. It had been new in 1929 and lasted until 1935. *(Senior Transport Archive)*

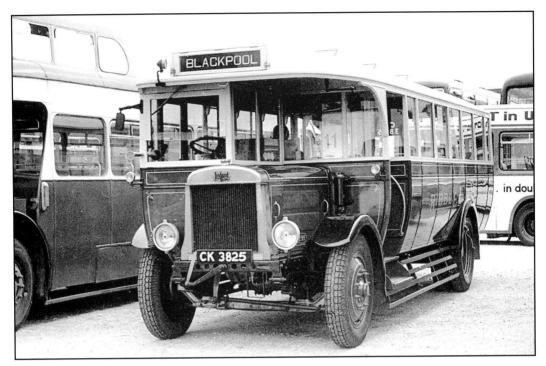

## LEYLAND PLSC LIONS

**Above:** The PLSC Lion, a design masterpiece which stood out head and shoulders above the Leviathans and Lionesses in the immediate pre-Rackham period at Leyland, formed the backbone of fleets large and small all over the country. Ribble bought large numbers of both the PLSC1 and the longer PLSC3 versions. Number **295** (**CK3825**) was a 1927 PLSC1 with Leyland 31-seat bodywork. It was withdrawn in 1938, did time with a fairground showman and then as a static caravan, before being rescued for preservation. GeoffreyAtkins photographed it at Derby in September 1983. This bus is now part of the Manchester Museum of Transport collection. **Below:** Number **460** (**CK3918**), from the following year, was a PLSC3 32-seater, which lasted with Ribble until 1939. Eleven years of service with the first operator was exceptional for vehicles built in the mid 1920s; such longevity did much to establish Leyland during those economically depressed times. *(Senior Transport Archive)*

## LEYLAND TD1 TITANS

Rackham's masterpiece (or, rather, one of them), the Leyland Titan, brought double-deck operation to new heights of sophistication. Its low height and nimble performance allowed it to be used in circumstances unthinkable for its lumbering, under-powered predecessors of any make. In a view *(above)*, dating from 26th May 1930, Ribble's new TD1 No. **752** (**CK4216**), a 48-seater with enclosed staircase, was out in the country on the Blackburn to Wigan via Chorley service. On the following 28th March *(below)* a trio of Ribble TD1s had conveyed racegoers to the 1931 Grand National at Aintree. Number **822** (**CK4272**) is the first in line; it and the other pair were all from the same 1930 batch of lowbridge 48-seaters. *(Both: Senior Transport Archive)*

## COACHING & COACH STATIONS

Geoffrey Atkins took a great interest in long-distance coaching operations in the early 1930s. At that time such services were in their infancy, although many had been established before the Road Traffic Act, 1930, came into force with effect from 1st April 1931. Much planning and attention to detail was producing ever more luxurious vehicles on some imaginative services linking towns, cities, and even villages, by swift journeys that had otherwise been a logistical nightmare to contemplate. Hand-in-glove with the development of the Leyland Titan double-decker came the single-deck Tiger, at that time often to what we would describe as service-bus specification, as in the example *(above)* from 1929, which was a 26-seat TS2 numbered **604** (**CK4086**) in the Ribble fleet. The high-backed seat was then a thing of the future, however, as was universal provision of such things as curtains and luggage compartments, and buses such as CK4086 provided comfort, if not exactly luxury, on some quite lengthy runs. *(Senior Transport Archive)*

>>> *Pages 14 and 15:* Geoffrey Atkins was a frequent visitor to Manchester, and readers of earlier volumes in this series, particularly *Tyne-Tees-Mersey* and *North Western*, will know that a fine series of portraits at Lower Mosley Street, Manchester, was produced over some five decades or so showing many aspects of the express coaching scene in the North-West. In these two views of Lower Mosley Street, the first shows it in 1934 before the central loading barriers were built; the second is from the following year after the rebuilding work. Ribble Leyland coaches are prominent in both views. In the 1934 view can be seen, across the road, the rival coach station operated by Finglands. The banners were advertising competing services to London and Glasgow, as well as services to Great Yarmouth, Torquay, Nottingham, Blackpool, Blackburn and North Wales. In 1937 Omnibus Stations Limited, owners of Lower Mosley Street coach station, bought the competing site.

14

15

## LEYLAND TS2 TIGERS

*Above:* One of the 1928 TS2 Tigers, No. **480** (**CK3938**), at Lower Mosley Street in June 1934. There were 40 in the batch. The body was the standard Leyland service bus product of the time, fitted out with 29 more comfortable seats for what would, much later, come to be referred to as "dual-purpose" use. CK3938 was withdrawn in 1938 and went on to work for five years in the Western SMT fleet.

*Below:* 1930's TS2s included No. **838** (**CK4298**), a Leyland-bodied 26-seater, again intended for express use. Luggage racks were fitted, but the seating was rather plain. (NB. The number shown, B837, was the body number, *not* the fleet number.) The six-cylinder, petrol-engined vehicle would nonetheless have been smooth and comfortable, more so, probably, than later oil-engined vehicles, however comfortable the latter's seating might be. *(Senior Transport Archive)*

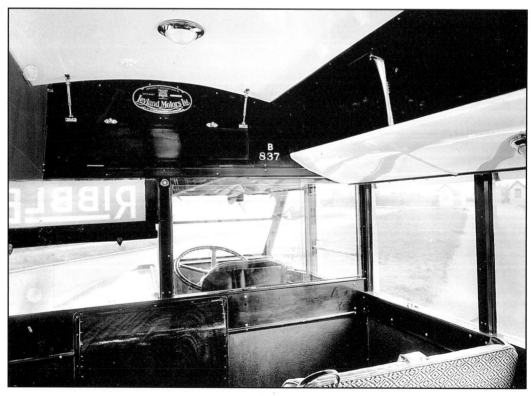

## LEYLAND TS3 TIGERS

*Above:* Number **1084** (**CK4441**), a Leyland-bodied 26-seat TS3 Tiger dating from 1931, threads its way up a narrow street in Ilfracombe in June 1931, on its way, "express", to Liverpool. The picture was taken a few weeks after the commencement of the Ilfracombe to Liverpool service by the Merseyside Touring Company jointly with Greyhound Motor Services, of Bristol. Ribble had lent the Tiger to Merseyside to operate the service until the Merseyside operation was fully integrated into Ribble the following September.

*Below:* There were 52 TS3s in 1931, all with 26-seat bodies and roof-mounted luggage racks. Although the seats were not high-backed, they were sumptuous and well spaced-out, and the vehicles were ideally suited to express work, leaving the Lions, with up to 35 seats, to cope with the more local stage-carriage work. This is No. **1117** (**CK4474**), seen at Tithebarn Street bus station, Preston in 1931. *(Senior Transport Archive)*

## LEYLAND LT LIONS

*Above:* The successful PLSC Lion was felt to be in need of updating and the LT series was the result. The LT1 appeared in the Ribble fleet in 1929. Number **598** (**CK4080**) was one of a batch of 32, all with 30-seat front-entrance Leyland bodywork. It was photographed on 20th March 1931. *(Senior Transport Archive)*

*Below:* On the same day, one of the 1930 LT2 Lions was captured by the camera on its way to Longridge. Number **803** (**CK4283**) showed some tidying up of body detail, particularly the side windows, when compared with No. 598 above. Both these Lions were withdrawn from service in 1939, went on to new owners, and survived into the postwar period. *(Senior Transport Archive)*

## LEYLAND TS6 TIGERS

*Above:* The trappings of luxury - high-backed seats and curtains - had arrived by 1933. That year saw a batch of 36 TS6 Tigers thus equipped. There were two versions: the 18 bodied by Leyland as 31-seaters are represented by No. **1370** (**CK4724**), seen at Lower Mosley Street, Manchester, in May 1935. Noteworthy are the "via" locations displayed in the nearside-front window.

*Below:* The remaining 18 were 26-seaters bodied by English Electric. In another Lower Mosley Street view from the camera of Geoffrey Atkins, No. **1384** (**CK4738**) is illustrated in a June 1934 shot. Both these coaches were among those withdrawn on the outbreak of war in 1939 and requisitioned by the War Department in July 1940. Neither returned to Ribble.

### LEYLAND TS7 TIGERS

*Above:* For 1937's large intake of TS7 Tiger coaches the order for bodywork was again split, this time between English Electric and Duple; each produced an attractive 31-seat front-entrance design. Number **1451 (RN7618)** was one of the English Electric versions. It is seen, in a postwar view not long before its withdrawal in 1950, on a football private hire to Derby. This photograph, from a postcard in the Geoffrey Atkins collection, was taken by Roy Marshall.

*Below:* Number **1500 (RN7750)** represents the Duple version of this classic ensemble. It was at Lower Mosley Street, Manchester, in August 1936. In 1950, a number of these vehicles were rebodied as 8ft-wide coaches with new Duple bodies and fitted with Leyland diesel engines; No. 1500 was not one of them, and was withdrawn in that year. The letter "R" within a belted scroll in this prewar picture contrasts with the simple fleetname in small script seen in the picture above.

The elegant lines of the Duple body are well shown in this angle of No. **1539 (RN7789)**, photographed on 19th October 1936. This was another 1950 withdrawal. *(Senior Transport Archive)*

Some of 1937's Duple-bodied TS7s were similarly rebodied and re-engined in 1950. **RN7994**, originally numbered 1650, was renumbered **767** for its new role and lasted until 1960. It was at Llandudno in June 1951.

## LEYLAND CHEETAHS

*Above:* Some generally similar 31-seat coach bodies built by Brush, of Loughborough, appeared on Leyland LZ2 Cheetah chassis in 1936 and Geoffrey Atkins was once again on hand to record them when brand new at Manchester's Lower Mosley Street coach station. Number **1573 (RN7829)** had entered service in July 1936; the photograph was taken in August. It was withdrawn in 1951.

*Below:* Number **2275 (RN8840)** was a later Cheetah model, based on the LZ5 chassis, again with 31-seat coachwork by Brush, which joined the fleet in July 1939. This one was a 1952 withdrawal, having been renumbered 1194 the previous year. Prominent on the rear panel is the Dewandre power-braking warning triangle, also visible on pages 24/5. *(Senior Transport Archive)*

## LEYLAND TD4 TITANS

*Above and << opposite page:* While all these exotic coaches were flooding into the fleet in the mid 1930s, additions to the more mundane double-deck department were being catered for by the provision of Leyland Titan TD4 chassis fitted with lowbridge bodywork. The examples illustrated - both with Leyland metal-framed bodies - are No. **1490** (**RN7673**) of 1935 and No. **1597** (**RN7803**) of the following year. The latter was withdrawn in 1953, but No. 1490 was remarkably long-lived, surviving into 1960 when it was withdrawn with the fleet number 2781, which it had been given in January 1956. Other TD4s were bodied by Burlingham, Roe and Eastern Counties, possibly after Leyland's metal-framed product had been found to have serious problems and in many cases to have needed extensive remedial rebuilding work. *(Senior Transport Archive)*

## DENNIS ACES

**Above:** Nineteen-thirty-four was a quiet year for new vehicles. There were a dozen Leyland TD3 Titans, bodied by English Electric, and six 20-seat Dennis Ace buses, also with English Electric bodywork. Number **1415** (**CK4885**), with Ulverston in its destination screen, serves to illustrate the batch. *(G H F Atkins Collection)*

**Below:** A single Dennis Ace was added in 1936, again a 20-seater, this time with bodywork by Dennis. In this wartime view, No. **1657** (**RN7858**) was in full blackout regalia of white-painted mudguard edges and masked headlamps. Strangely, the light alongside the destination screen had not been masked. Perhaps it had simply been disconnected. These little buses were withdrawn in 1948 and 1951. *(G H F Atkins Collection)*

By the time of 1938's Titans, the model designation had moved on to TD5, a large batch of which were bodied by Burlingham or Brush. Number **1772** (**RN8156**) is seen at Liverpool in May 1957, with the Eastern Coach Works body it had received in 1948. The rebodied vehicle was withdrawn in 1959. Ribble's in-house advertising - "Be Safe and Save with Ribble" - might well have been aimed at the competing railway services.

## ALEXANDER BODIES

*Above:* The inflow of Titan TD5s continued in 1939: lowbridge 53-seaters with either Burlingham or Brush bodywork. Many of them had their lives prolonged by the postwar rebodying programme, including No. **2058** (**RN8623**), which received an Alexander body of the same specification in 1949. In this view, it was at St Helens in June 1956, four years before its withdrawal. Happily, one of these buses survives in preservation.

*Below:* Number 2043 (**RN8608**) was another of the Alexander rebodies. It was withdrawn in 1961 and sold to Barton Transport, of Chilwell, for whom it ran until the end of 1965. It was scrapped in January 1966. In this Mount Street, Nottingham, photograph taken in May 1962, the vehicle is seen in Barton livery.

## WARTIME UTILITY GUYS & DAIMLERS

*Above:* When war broke out in 1939, an immediate effect for the bus industry was that all bus and coach construction was halted by Government order. Later, the completion was authorised of vehicles that could be manufactured from parts already in existence: the "unfrozen" buses. For the rest of the war, Guy, Daimler, Bristol and Bedford were instructed to build buses to an austere, utility design and these were allocated to operators according to need. Ribble took both Guys and Daimlers. Number **2406 (ACK756)** was a Guy Arab II with a Duple lowbridge body which came in 1943. It was withdrawn in 1955. This photograph shows the bus as rebuilt by Bond, of Wythenshawe, in the early 1950s. *Below:* This 1944 Brush-bodied lowbridge Daimler CWA6 was never in the Ribble fleet although there is a strong link. **ACK837** was new in 1944 to Viking Motors (Preston) Limited, and would have been in service alongside Ribble vehicles. The Viking business, not including the vehicles, was taken over by Ribble on 11th November 1952. ACK837 was sold to a new owner in Wales and disappears from recorded history around 1954. *(Roy Marshall; Senior Transport Archive)*

## THE POSTWAR LEYLAND TITAN PD1

*Above:* Number **2449** (**ARN183**) was the first bus built to postwar peacetime standards to enter the Ribble fleet. One of a batch of 31 which were delivered in 1946 and 1947, it was a Titan PD1 with 56-seat highbridge bodywork by Burlingham. These vehicles had Leyland 7.4-litre engines when new. Leyland O600 engines were substituted when the buses were about two years old, and the 7.4s fitted to prewar Tigers and Cheetahs.

*Below:* The last of the 1946 double-deckers was No. **2466** (**ARN200**), which was put into service in December. Both it and No. 2449 were withdrawn in 1958; each found a new owner and lasted into the mid 1960s. These photographs were taken in Liverpool in May 1957, by which time the destination indicators had been altered to the later standard and only one cream band was specified.

## THE POSTWAR LEYLAND TITAN PD1

*Above:* The next vehicle numerically, No. **2467** (**ARN201**), was the first of the 1947 deliveries, entering service in January. Its history of engine-changes, withdrawal and disposal was similar to that of the vehicles described on the previous page. Before being sold in 1958, the 1946/7 PD1s regained 7.4-litre engines, transferred from 1947 originally Brush-bodied PD1As (which had been rebodied by Burlingham - *see page 32* - in 1955). The 1955 Burlingham rebodies were then equipped with the O600 engines. *Below:* Leyland won the order to body part of 1947's batch of PD1A Titans. Highbridge 56-seaters resulted, exemplified by No. **2470** (**BCK413**), seen at Liverpool in May 1957, as was ARN201 above. The other body contract for the 1947 PD1As went to Brush and was for lowbridge units. These two buses combine the later destination screen standard with the earlier two-cream-band livery arrangement.

## BURLINGHAM REBODIES

*Above:* Some of the Brush lowbridge Titan PD1As of 1947 were rebodied in 1955 following the discovery of rot caused by poor timber framing. The contract went to Burlingham, who produced 8ft-wide metal-framed 53-seat lowbridge units with platform doors. In 1958 the rebodied vehicles were further upgraded, as described on the previous page, when they were fitted with Leyland O600 engines taken from the 1946/7 Burlingham highbridge PD1s. Number **2484 (BCK427)** was at Bolton in August 1957.

*Below:* The offside angle of the 1955 Burlingham body design is shown on No. **2513 (BCK456)**, photographed in July 1956 at Lower Mosley Street, Manchester, as it waited to take up a departure timing on service X60 to Blackpool - a duty at that date often assigned to a "White Lady".

## DEBUT OF THE "WHITE LADY"

Perhaps the biggest problem faced by the operator wishing to attract traffic to express journeys was that single-deckers could not cope with loadings and heavy duplication was required. One option in the search for a solution was to introduce double-deck "coaches" which, in fact, might differ internally little from service-bus standard, however exotic and eye-catching the exterior might be. This was much the case with Ribble's celebrated "White Ladies", which came in two varieties. The first 30, delivered in 1948/9, were PD1/3 Titans with Burlingham 49-seat bodies with full-width fronts and platform doors. Numbers **1223 (BRN283)** *(above)* and **1216 (BRN276)** were at Lower Mosley Street, Manchester, in July 1956 and May 1952. They were respectively working the X43 to Skipton and the X60 to Blackpool.

# THE NEW EXPRESS

The Company certainly thought much of the "White Lady" concept and proudly published a full, illustrated description in its Staff Bulletin. It is difficult to conclude with certainty either way whether these 49-seaters, specifically because of their livery, embellishments and luggage racks, attracted passengers from less flamboyant machines: the hard-headed Lancastrian off to Blackpool for the day, or for a week's holiday, probably cared little for the looks of his transport so long as it delivered him to the resort with the minimum of fuss and delay. By way of contrast, the North Western Road Car Company, often working jointly with Ribble on this type of service, provided standard Leyland-bodied Titans in normal service-bus livery on which the only concession to "express" status was the fitment of platform doors. *(Keith Healey Collection)*

# SERVICE VEHICLE

ON Wednesday, 23rd June, the Directors of the Company made an examination of the first of a number of new double-decked vehicles designed specially for use on express services. The photograph on this page shows five of the Directors (unfortunately Mr. C. H. Sutherland had to leave before it was taken) together with the General Manager, Mr. H. Bottomley, and the Chief Engineer, Mr. A. S. Woodgate. It was taken on the top deck of the vehicle after a trial run from Blackpool to Preston.

On Friday, 25th June, a demonstration run was made for representatives of the Press who also had an opportunity of examining the vehicle in great detail. Their praise of it as being a great advance in road passenger transport and a sign of initiative and enterprise, providing as it does improved facilities

Luggage accommodation is provided at each side of the main gangway near the entrance to the lower saloon, in a well under the staircase on the rear platform, under the floor of the rear platform, to the nearside of the driver's cab which extends the full width of the vehicle, on a heavy luggage rack running the full length of the lower saloon on the nearside and on a light rack to the rear of the upper saloon.

There is an exceptionally good forward view for passengers travelling in the lower saloon and a twin sunshine roof is provided to improve travel conditions in the upper saloon, the sliding portions being panelled with "Perspex".

In the cold weather, an efficient heater will supply warm air to both lower and upper saloons and ample ventilation is provided by sliding windows with additional ventilation in summer through the radiator ducts when cold air is substituted for warm air.

Extra width of seating space per passenger has been made possible by taking advantage of the in-

Left to right : Mr. H. BOTTOMLEY, General Manager, Mr. J. W. WOMAR, Managing Director, Mr. W. E. YATES, Director, Mr. E. L. TAYLOR, Director, Mr. R. P. BEDDOW, Chairman, Mr. T. W. ROYLE, Director, Mr. A. S. WOODGATE, Chief Engineer.

for passengers, is, we hope, only a foretaste of the approval our patrons will give when numbers of this type of vehicle are put into service shortly.

It has been designed by Mr. A. S. Woodgate, the Chief Engineer, and it is intended to cater for journeys of up to 60 or 70 miles on such express services as East Lancashire to Blackpool and Manchester, Liverpool, East Lancashire and Manchester to Blackpool and Morecambe and Blackpool to Morecambe.

The exterior of the vehicle leaves little to be desired for elegance and modernity and, within the scope prescribed by constructional regulations laid down by the Minister of Transport and the tendency for standardisation in chassis production, it has many new and improved features.

The chassis is the standard Leyland P.D.1 type and the body has been built by Burlinghams.

crease from 7 ft. 6 ins. to 8ft. of the overall width of the vehicle. The width of the gangway remains as on standard vehicles but the extra width of the seats prevents the "over-flowing" of passengers into the gangway.

Our General Manager conceived the idea for this type of vehicle, firstly on account of the heavily increased demand for medium-distance express travel and secondly as a means of combating steeply rising costs, in this way assisting to provide an excellent standard of service without resorting to increased fares. To achieve this when operating costs have almost doubled since the outbreak of War (wages alone have increased by 75 per cent) is making a valuable contribution to the National efforts to stem the rising tide of prices because if fares were increased, practically every worker's cost of living would be affected.

1. Placing luggage in the space behind the wheel-arch.
2. Excellent forward view for passengers in the lower saloon.
3. Pleasing and unusual front view.
4. General view—note the attractive lines, rounded windows and increased visibility for the driver.
5. Placing luggage in the compartment under the platform.
6. Upper saloon, showing longer and roomier seats and transparent sliding roof panels.

When these vehicles were new they carried the fleet numbers 2518 - 2547; in 1951 they were renumbered 1201 - 1230. The featured vehicle in this contemporary Ribble article was No. **2518 (BRN261)**, the first numerically, and the first to enter service, in June 1948. It shows the original frontal treatment below the windscreen, which was found to be inadequate for engine-cooling and was replaced by the design seen on Nos 1223 and 1216 *(see page 33)*. The "White Lady" fleet was expanded in 1950/1 with a further 20, fitted with East Lancashire Coachbuilders bodies *(see page 36)*, and the principle found new expression in the rear-engined Leyland Atlantean coaches of 1959-62 *(see pages 51/2)*.

<< *Opposite page:* The East Lancs-bodied PD2/3 version of the "White Lady" is represented by No. **1231** (**DCK202**). In this May 1957 Lower Mosley Street view, the vehicle is standing in front of one of the earlier Burlingham versions. The similarity was remarkable: perhaps the easiest way of telling them apart at a quick glance was by the panel between the rearmost side window and the platform, although a second glance would reveal the four- rather than five-bay construction of the East Lancs version. East Lancs bodies were rare in the Ribble fleet, only three others being recorded: on 1942 "unfrozen" Leyland Titans.

*Above:* A red "White Lady" with luggage racks removed on the lower deck, thus allowing an increased seating capacity of 53. This conversion was done in 1956 on No. **1225** (**BRN285**), formerly No. 2542; the whole batch of 30 was similarly converted between 1955 and 1958. Number 1225 was at Lower Mosley Street in June 1958.

*Below:* Sentinel-Beadle SB four-cylinder-engined integral bus No. **278** (**CRN211**) was delivered in May 1949 as fleet number 2722. Leyland must have been dismayed (as must AEC) to see an underfloor-engined Sentinel at the Commercial Motor Show in 1948 in advance of the Olympic, Royal Tiger and Regal IV. The dismay probably turned to outright shock when Ribble not only ordered one but ran it in service past Leyland's factory gates. Perhaps it was just Ribble's way of telling Leyland to get a move on with its own underfloor-engined chassis, for No. 2722 was not trouble-free and although Ribble bought five production models (by then known as the STC4) in 1950 and 14 of the six-cylinder STC6 version in 1951, that was the end of this brief non-Leyland fling. The Ribble Sentinels had a full lifespan, however, mostly in the Carlisle area, and were not withdrawn until 1962/3. (*Roy Marshall*)

## THE LEYLAND PD2 TITAN

*Above:* In three years from 1948 to 1950 Ribble bought 227 new Leyland PD2 Titans. The first were lowbridge Leyland-bodied 53-seaters in the late summer of 1948. Typical of them in intermediate external condition, with two cream bands and the later style of destination screen arrangement, was No. **2599** (**CCK374**), seen at Liverpool in May 1957. It was withdrawn in 1962.

*Below:* Number 2588 (**CCK363**) was another 1962 withdrawal and was one of five to be purchased by Barton Transport, of Chilwell. The others were ex-Ribble 2567, 2578, 2587 and 2590. CCK363 became Barton fleet number **955**, and in this April 1963 view it was at Mount Street, Nottingham. The Barton livery, a good deal more complicated than that of Ribble, suited the Leyland body well.

## THE LEYLAND PD2 TITAN

The PD2 story took an unexpected turn in 1949 when a batch of 8ft-wide Leyland-bodied highbridge examples arrived. They had been ordered by the Cape Town Tramways Company, South Africa, but were diverted to the home market. Some entered service with Capetown destination screens and all had more opening windows than usual for UK-market vehicles. The number of opening windows had been reduced by the time of these Liverpool views of No. **2641** (**CCK629**) taken in May 1957. It is thought that this bus had Ribble's later standard-pattern destination screens from new. Number 2641 lasted until 1963 and after withdrawal ran for an independent before going for scrap in May 1966.

## BRUSH BODIES FOR THE PD2 TITAN

*Above:* Further variety in 1949 came from a batch of Brush-bodied 8ft-wide lowbridge 53-seaters. There were 31, delivery of which spread over into 1950. In this April 1954 photograph, No. **2681** (**CCK657**) is seen in Blackburn. These appear to have been the first batch to have the new standard destination indicators.

*Below:* Number **2672** (**CCK648**) was in Darwen on the same day. These buses were 1960 withdrawals, not lasting quite as long as some of their Leyland-bodied contemporaries. Number 2672 later ran for the South Notts Bus Company Limited, of Gotham, and 2681 went much further south, to Hedingham & District (D A McGregor), of Sible Hedingham.

## THE LEYLAND PD2 TITAN

*Above:* In 1950 the stream of PD2s continued. Leyland lowbridge 53-seat bodies were specified for a batch of 50 of the PD2/3 variant. In another of Geoffrey Atkins's May 1957 series of Ribble portraits taken in Liverpool, No. **2738** (**CRN831**) was on the Crosby service. In terms of mass appeal in 1957, a £75,000 win on Vernons Pools would perhaps equal £1 million from the lottery in 2001.

*Below:* Just over six years earlier, on a dank, dismal Manchester day in March 1951, No. **2776** (**CRN869**) was displaying a livery variation compared with 2738 above, in that the lower cream band continued round the bonnet and cab-front. These buses were withdrawn in 1964 and 1965 and sold to a Salford dealer. Neither ran in public service again, although 2776 worked for the contractor John Laing & Son Ltd for a short time.

## MORE UNDERFLOOR ENGINES AND PLATFORM DOORS

*Above:* In late 1950 and 1951 the first Leyland underfloor-engined single-deckers entered the Ribble fleet. They were based on the integral Leyland-MCW Olympic HR44. A batch of 30, numbered 248 - 277 under the new numbering scheme introduced in 1950, had front-entrance 44-seat bodywork. Number **277 (DRN141)** was photographed at Knott End in May 1957 on its way to Lancaster on service 80.

*Below:* The 14 six-cylinder STC6 Sentinels were also 44-seaters, with bodies built by Sentinel. This one is ex-No. 287 **(DRN344)**, seen after its withdrawal and sale. It was with its second subsequent owner and was in use as a mobile café at Broad Marsh, Nottingham, in September 1966.

## MORE PD2/3 TITANS

*Above:* Nineteen-fifty's PD2/3 intake culminated in a batch of 50 lowbridge Leyland-bodied 50-seaters fitted with platform doors. As fleet numbers 1301 - 1350, they started the 1950 numbering scheme's series for double-deck buses. Number **1315 (DRN255)** was at Lower Mosley Street, Manchester, in May 1952.

*Below:* This splendidly nostalgic scene in Kendal in the 1950s includes another of the 1950 PD2/3 Titans, No. **1343 (DRN283)**, threading its way gently between a Vauxhall cabriolet of decidedly vintage aspect and oncoming traffic, which just happened to be being led by Ribble's No. **953 (GCK288)**, one of the 1954 Tiger Cubs fitted with centre-entrance Burlingham Seagull bodies *(see page 46). (Senior Transport Archive)*

## LEYLAND ROYAL TIGERS

Despite the earlier purchase of the Sentinels and the Leyland Olympics, the restocking of the single-deck fleet began in earnest with Leyland Royal Tigers. The majority of those ordered were coaches, including no fewer than 145 with a new metal-framed body by Leyland. These centre-entrance 41-seaters are epitomised by No. **812 (DRN734)** *(<< opposite page)*, which was brand new in May 1951 at Matlock Bath on excursion work. Five years later, in March 1956, No. **874 (ECK154)** *(above)* was at Huntingdon Street, Nottingham, "on hire to North Western" on an express journey to Manchester. It would then continue to Blackpool as part of the through-linking arrangement *(see page 58)*. The lower panels at the front had been restyled to include the spotlight. Leyland's body for the service bus version of the Royal Tiger was very different and verged on the austere. It did the job for which it was intended, though, and all 110 Ribble examples lasted well into the 1960s. Number **384 (ERN707)** was at Liverpool *(below)* in May 1957. The writer had the pleasure of driving one of these buses, ex-No. 377 (ERN700), after it had been converted by Ribble and donated to the Windermere Cheshire Home.

## THE LEYLAND TIGER CUB

*Above:* The last Royal Tiger coaches for Ribble were a batch of 20 in 1953/4 with Burlingham Seagull centre-entrance bodies sumptuously fitted out with 32 generously spaced seats. The second of the batch, No. **927** (**FCK427**), was photographed in Cheapside, Nottingham, in August 1958.

*Below:* The Royal Tiger, sturdy and dependable as it undoubtedly was, was found, as was AEC's Regal IV, somewhat heavily engineered for the work required of it, and the more lightly constructed Tiger Cub was introduced (AEC's answer was the Reliance). The first Ribble coaches on this new chassis carried externally similar centre-entrance Burlingham Seagull bodies, which seated 41. Number **949** (**GCK284**) is illustrated when brand new. *(Senior Transport Archive)*

## THE LEYLAND TIGER CUB

*Above:* Burlingham Seagull bodies were supplied to Ribble on Tiger Cub chassis from 1954 to 1958. The later examples had a revised side-window design and flat, one-piece windscreens as well as front entrances. All these features are displayed on No. **989 (LCK703)**, seen at Maid Marian Way, Nottingham, in October 1958.

*Below:* There were 50 Tiger Cub service buses in 1954, bodied as front-entrance 44-seaters by Saunders-Roe, of Anglesey. The harmonious lines of the body valiantly overcame Ribble's rather dull all-red livery, and it was sad to see the coachbuilder go out of business soon afterwards, especially as their bodies turned out to be of outstanding reliability. Number **443 (FCK875)** was at Lower Mosley Street, Manchester, in June 1959, waiting to leave for Clitheroe on service X23. Similar vehicle FCK 884 still exists in 2001 in preservation.

In the meantime, the Titan model designation had moved to PD2/12 for a batch of Leyland-bodied 53-seaters with platform doors delivered in 1952. These were the last traditional lowbridge buses bought by Ribble. Number **1375 (ECK945)** was in a damp Bolton bus station in June 1956, working the X60 to Blackpool.

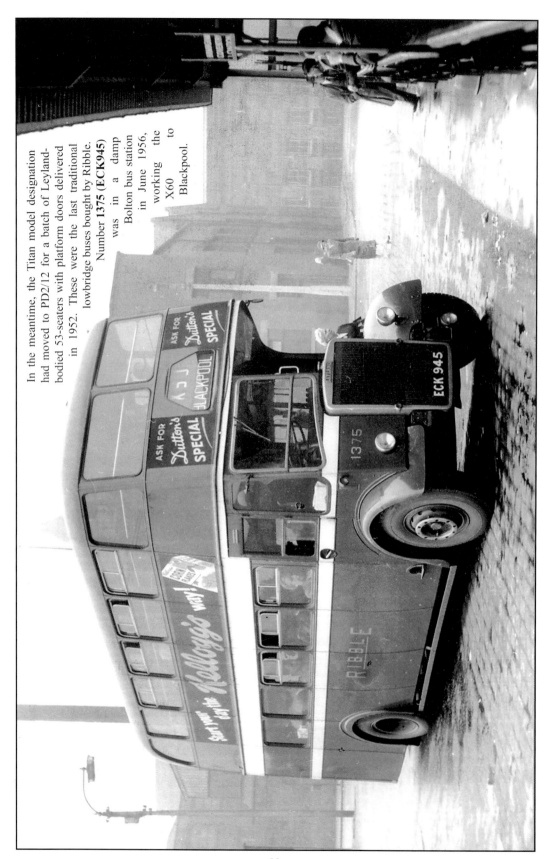

## THE CLOSURE OF LEYLAND'S COACHBUILDING FACTORY

In 1955/6 Ribble, and many another operator throughout the United Kingdom (and, indeed, the rest of the world), had to come to terms with the disappearance of Leyland as a coachbuilder. Quite why this happened has never been satisfactorily explained. The suggestion that the factory floorspace was needed for building cabs for Leyland Comet lorries was surely not the whole story. Be that as it may, Ribble had 120 Titans on order, of either PD2/12 (with vacuum brakes) or PD2/13 (air-assisted brakes) types, and bodywork had to be sourced elsewhere. In the event the work was shared between Metro-Cammell and Burlingham. One of the former's bodies, which were built to the Orion shape but not specifically as lightweight constructions, is seen *(above)* on No. **1382** (**HCK463**), pictured at St Helens in June 1956. This bus was one of those with platform doors; others in the batch had open platforms. The Burlingham design is exemplified by No. **1458** (**JCK533**) *(below)*, at Lower Mosley Street, Manchester, in May 1965. Again, there were versions with and without platform doors and this was one of those with them. The Dulux advertisement heralded the start of the great DIY movement.

## THE LEYLAND PD3

*Above:* After a good deal of lobbying from operators, including Barton, of Chilwell, operating such vehicles in advance of the legislation, 30ft-long buses at last became legal in 1958. Leyland already had a 30ft Titan on the drawing board, known - logically - as the PD3. Ribble ordered a large batch which broke new ground in several other respects: the forward entrance with power-operated door and the fully fronted cab were the most obvious (the fully fronted "White Ladies" of a decade earlier had been designed thus to appeal as coaches, or at least as express buses, whereas the PD3s were plain service-buses from the outset). No fewer than 105 were bodied by Burlingham in 1957/8, represented by No. **1521 (KCK867)** at Blackpool's Coliseum coach station in May 1967.

*Below:* Number **1976 (MCK369)** was a near-contemporary Burlingham-bodied PD3, but of substantially different appearance. New in January 1959 to Scout Motor Services Limited, of Preston, it came into the Ribble fleet as late as 1968 when the Scout fleet was absorbed. Scout's share capital had been acquired in 1961, but the company was kept on as a subsidiary until October 1968, when the fleet was divided between Ribble and Standerwick, also a subsidiary. Number 1976 was at Manchester in August 1969.

## THE LEYLAND ATLANTEAN

The Leyland Atlantean, a prototype of which had appeared at the 1956 Commercial Motor Show, ought to have revolutionised the British bus industry rather more promptly than it did. The initial PDR1 models, however, were prone to unreliability, and some years elapsed before the revamped AN68 really took hold of the market. Ribble was among the earliest customers, placing in service both full- and low-height service buses and - a sensation at the time - a fleet of motorway coaches baptised "Gay Hostesses" in an age more innocent than ours when such a word could be used with its proper meaning and a complete lack of innuendo. Number **1693** (**NRN593**) *(above)* was a 1960 full-height 78-seater (and *that* was the Atlantean's crucial selling point: no other manufacturer could then offer as high a seating capacity), photographed in Manchester in May 1963. "Gay Hostess" No. **1256** (**NRN605**) *(below)* was in the same place exactly a year earlier. These double-deck coaches could certainly eat up the miles; on at least one occasion one was clocked by a police car crew at 85mph on the southern end of the M1 and apparently such speeds were commonplace.

<< *Opposite page:* Atlantean No. **1277** (**RRN426**) was one of a 1962 batch of 20, less sophisticated than the "Gay Hostesses" but slightly more so than the service bus version. The specification and livery were designed for duties formerly carried out by the PD1 and PD2 Titan "White Ladies" of a generation earlier. Number 1277 was at Lower Mosley Street, Manchester, in April 1971.

## LONGER COACHES, TOO ...

*This page:* The products of Thomas Harrington, of Hove, came to the Ribble fleet in the 1960s in short (on Leopard L2 chassis) and long (on Leopard PSU3 chassis) versions. The former is represented *(above)* by Nos **1025** and **1039** (**PCK607/621**) at Haworth, Yorkshire, in May 1971, whilst the longer version, in the shape of No. **710** (**TCK710**), was at Huntingdon Street, Nottingham *(below)*, in March 1970. These were respectively 1961 and 1963 deliveries. Number 710 had just arrived in Nottingham from Great Yarmouth on hire to Trent, and would continue to Manchester and Blackpool. By the time it reached its destination it would have had three different crews: Trent, North Western and Ribble *(see page 58)*.

## THE 36ft-LONG COACH IS ESTABLISHED

*Above:* When Ribble acquired the share capital of Scout, it also took over an outstanding order for six PSU3/3RT Leopards. Duple Northern coachwork was fitted to these, the first 36ft-long coaches to enter the Ribble fleet; they predated the first of the longer Harringtons by four months. The picture, featuring No. **702** (**SCK867**), the second of the six, was taken at Llandudno in July 1966.

*Below:* Plaxton succeeded Duple and Harrington as suppliers of 36ft-long coaches. Two quite different designs, both named "Panorama", appeared in the 1963-5 period. The earlier, a clean, unfussy creation, which emphasised the length, is seen on No. **758** (**TRN758**) at, appropriately, Scarborough, in August 1965. It had worked in on the Liverpool to Scarborough service, operated jointly with the West Yorkshire Road Car Company.

## COACHWORK FROM CAMBRIDGE

Marshall, of Cambridge, built some dual-purpose 49-seaters on the Leopard PSU3 chassis in 1964 and 1965. The "dual-purpose" concept is infuriatingly difficult to define: such vehicles were not necessarily any less comfortable than those classed as "coaches". It seemed to be a question more of appearance: luxurious seating and luggage racks in a shell the same shape as that of a service bus, and fitted with driver-controlled power-operated doors, could be used on either stage carriage or express services with equal facility. Hence the bus-shell dual-purpose vehicles were usually in a livery more akin to the coach fleet, as demonstrated by Nos **764/71** (**TRN764/71**) in June 1967. They were respectively at Lower Mosley Street, Manchester *(above)*, and Lord Street bus station, Southport *(below)*. The latter was a former railway station enterprisingly put to new public transport use rather than being given over to yet another car park. The two vehicles, despite being from the same 1964 batch (and photographed in the same month), had differing front panel arrangements. The lower picture shows the original style.

## THE FEDERATION STANDARD

The BET Federation, with its enormous purchasing power, had been, since before the Second World War, in a position to commission bodywork to its own design from several different coachbuilders. By the mid-1960s, the Federation standard was a 36ft-long 53-seater that was adaptable, as we saw on the last page, in that it could form the base for vehicles equipped to dual-purpose specification. The basic unit, however, was less glamorous and when, as with these Ribble examples, it was turned out in a dark livery unrelieved by either cream band or aluminium moulding, it was to some eyes rather unattractive. The reason given for the plain livery was that it was a cost-cutting exercise: it was cheaper not to have to mask off parts of the body in order to spray the rest another colour. This is strange: presumably today's operators (Stagecoach and FirstBus spring to mind) are no less cost-conscious, and yet they commission "explosion-in-a-paint-factory" liveries which are complicated in the extreme. Ribble's Federation 53-seaters are represented by 1964's Marshall-bodied No. **533** (**UCK533**) at Barnsley in June of that year *(above)*, and No. **591** (**ARN591C**), a Weymann example dating from 1965, seen *(below)* at Parliament Street Bridge (over the former Great Central railway line), Nottingham, in September 1970. By then, the fleetname transfer had been simplified to a lower-case *sans serif* style with no underlining. This was an unusual vehicle for this express working, and had probably been a breakdown replacement at Preston or Bolton.

## MORE PLAXTON COACHES

The harmonious design of the Plaxton Panorama body on the 1963 maximum-length coaches *(see page 54)* was somewhat compromised on the 1965 Leopard 49-seaters from the Scarborough coachbuilder. Numbers **777** and **786 (ARN777/86C)** display a certain flamboyance, particularly at the rear of the first bay, where a thick pillar seemed to split the top half of the body into two unequal-length sections, and in the perhaps too generous application of aluminium mouldings below the first bay and the windscreen. The vehicles were nonetheless impressive in a rather aggressive way, and were splendid performers on Britain's growing motorway network. These photographs were taken in April 1967 at Nottingham Trent Bridge and in August 1965 at Scarborough.

## MORE DUAL-PURPOSE VEHICLES

The dual-purpose version of the BET Federation shell *(see page 55)* was also built by the Addlestone, Surrey, coachbuilder Weymann who, in 1965, supplied ten 49-seaters. The application of what was virtually the same livery as that on contemporary coaches and their use on express services clearly indicated their main role when new; in later life such designs were often "cascaded" onto more mundane duties, more easily achieved with this specification of body than with full coaches. Number **808 (ARN808C)** *(above)* was at Huntingdon Street, Nottingham, in August 1965, loading for the run to Manchester. This was the age of no opening windows and forced ventilation, a system that apparently needed augmenting by leaving the door open in May 1967 *(below)* as No. **815 (ARN815C)** passed through St Annes on its way to Blackpool. Ribble was not officially an operator on the X2 Nottingham to Manchester service, which was run by North Western jointly with Trent. Following complaints from passengers wishing to travel beyond Manchester via the X60 to Blackpool, and encountering problems with the X60 vehicles having insufficient room for their luggage, it was agreed that Ribble would participate in the service and that drivers would interchange. At Manchester the blind would be changed to show Blackpool as all through passengers would have been directed to the Ribble coach. The service could not be licensed as Nottingham to Blackpool with vehicles displaying "Blackpool" because Robin Hood Coaches, of Nottingham, ran such a service, objected to what North Western, Ribble and Trent were doing and would have strenuously opposed any application before the Traffic Commissioners to license such a service.

The early Atlanteans bought by Ribble had included some of the low-height version, which involved a rather clumsy sunken gangway arrangement at the rear of the upper deck: a layout not found entirely satisfactory in service. In the 1950s, the Bristol Lodekka had pioneered the principle of centre gangways on both decks within the overall height of a traditional lowbridge bus, thus obviating the latter's inconvenience of sunken gangways and four-in-a-row upper-deck seating. Ribble, as a BET operator, could not order the Lodekka, and had not been tempted by AEC's Bridgmaster or Renown, or by the Dennis Loline, all of them low-height designs which achieved the same result as the Lodekka. Thus, when Albion (part of Leyland Motors) made available the Lowlander - effectively a PD3 Titan with low frame-line and dropped-centre rear axle - Ribble in 1964/5 bought 16 fitted with distinctive fully fronted Alexander 72-seat bodies. Number **1863 (ARN863C)** was in Bolton bus station in August 1969.

## A NEW COACHBUILDER FOR DUAL-PURPOSE VEHICLES

*Above:* The by then well-tried concept of putting 49 more comfortable seats into a bus shell that normally took 53 service-bus seats was progressed in 1966-68. Marshall was again called upon for bodywork for two batches of Leyland Leopards, each of 14, in 1966 and 1967. Number **830 (CRN830D)** was the penultimate of the 1966 group. It was at Bolton bus station in May 1970, having been converted for one-man-operation in 1967.

*Below:* Thirty similar 1968 vehicles were bodied by Willowbrook, of Loughborough, a familiar name in other BET fleets but hitherto not represented at Ribble. Number **929 (FCK929F)** was brand new in April 1968 when photographed at Lower Mosley Street, Manchester, on the X43 service to Burnley.

## THE ATLANTEAN MAKES A COMEBACK

After having reverted to front-engined PD3s and Albion Lowlanders following not entirely satisfactory experience with some early Atlanteans, Ribble bought 25 PDR1/2 Atlanteans in 1966/67. By then the Daimler Fleetline was in full spate and attracting many orders away from Leyland. The Fleetline design did away with the clumsy sunken gangway inflicted on the low-height version of the PDR1/1 Atlantean; Leyland sought to duplicate this by negotiating to use Daimler's gearbox which, combined with a back axle of Albion Lowlander design, brought the Atlantean up to date. Ribble's PDR1/2s were bodied by Alexander (10) and Northern Counties (15). An example of each, Nos **1868** (**CRN868D**) and **1956** (**ECK956E**), are seen at Blackpool in May 1967 *(above)* and at Lower Mosley Street, Manchester, *(below)* in August 1971.

## THE FIRST RIBBLE BEDFORDS

*Above:* Before 1966, Ribble had never had a Bedford chassis in public service. In that year, ten Bedford VAM5s with Plaxton Panorama 9.5-metre coachwork were purchased. These noisy, front-engined, lightweight chassis with Bedford diesel engines were found wanting and were withdrawn and sold in 1969. Number **858** (**CRN858D**) was at Plymouth Hoe in July 1967.

## PLAXTON'S PANORAMA AGAIN REDESIGNED

*Below:* As we have seen *(see above and pages 54/7)*, Plaxton's Panorama went from a clean, unfussy outline to a visually unfortunate embellished version. At the 1968 Commercial Motor Show there were sighs of relief when the Scarborough firm unveiled the Panorama Elite, a crisp, shapely design that became - and remains - a timeless classic. Ribble's examples included 36-, 43- and 49-seaters on either 10- or 11-metre chassis. Illustrated is one of the 36-seaters, dating from 1970. Number **993** (**KCK993H**) was at Westwood coach park, Scarborough, with Oliver's Mount prominent in the background, in September 1973.

## RIBBLE BUYS BRISTOLS

There must have been some dismay at Leyland when the unthinkable happened in 1968 and Ribble began to order Bristol chassis in considerable quantities. Leyland had acquired a 25% shareholding in Bristol Commercial Vehicles in 1965, thus allowing the previously 100% state-owned vehicle manufacturer to seek orders outside the ranks of the state-owned operators. Leyland's management could hardly have foreseen local operator Ribble's defection, and it has been suggested that the affair was in part responsible for British Leyland becoming determined, given the chance, to close Bristol down, an outrage (in the eyes of many) which finally came about on 28th January 1983. Leyland had acquired the National Bus Company's interests - and therefore total control - in the Bristol chassis builder a mere two months earlier; the speed with which it then eliminated Bristol lends credence to the theory that such a move had been long planned and was carried out for reasons unconnected with Bristol's commercial viability. Leyland also closed down Eastern Coach Works, fearing - it is said - that Bristol/ECW products would take work away from Leyland's own factories: what confidence in their own products! There have, perhaps, been greater scandals in the sorry history of British industry, but surely not many. Ribble ordered single- and double-deckers and we illustrate RE types with Marshall and Eastern Coach Works bodies. Number **309 (LRN309J)** *(above)* was photographed in the charming town of Appleby, in August 1978. New in 1970, this Marshall-bodied 47-seater was by then carrying National Bus Company livery. The picture below, taken at Bolton in May 1973, illustrates ECW-bodied No. **357 (OCK357K)**, an April 1972 delivery. Both these buses had Leyland engines although some of Ribble's Bristols were Gardner-powered.

## NATIONAL BUS COMPANY COACHES

*Above:* Number **1061** (**822YEH**) was one of a pair of Plaxton-bodied L2T Leopards which Michelin Tyres Ltd had used as demonstrators for Michelin X tyres. New in January 1963, Ribble acquired them in November of that year. The photograph was taken at Grange Over Sands in May 1974.

*Below:* ECW-bodied Bristol RE No. **1012** (**PTF707L**) was a 1972 49-seater, seen in Bolton bus station in August 1974 on its way to Edinburgh.

## THE CARLISLE TRANSFER

>> *Opposite page:* ECW-bodied Bristols came via a different route when, on 5th January 1969, as one of the first acts of the National Bus Company, which had come into legal existence four days earlier, the Carlisle operation of United Automobile Services was transferred to Ribble. Of the United allocation of 24 vehicles, three elderly Bristol-engined KSW double-deckers were rejected but twenty-one 45-seat single-deckers were transferred, comprising five integrally constructed LSs with Gardner 5-cylinder engines, eleven five-cylinder MWs and five of the more powerful version of the MW with the Gardner 6LW engine. Illustrated are No. **262** (**632CHN**), one of the LS5Gs; and No. **272** (**5040HN**), an MW5G. These had been fleet numbers U232 and U640 in United's fleet. Withdrawals of the older examples began in 1970 but, although non-standard, the newest MW5G and all the six-cylinder examples ran until 1974. *(Photobus)*